Praise

Chet's insights on ideal clie⌐
are incredible! This book provides you with a mantra-like manifesto to find the clients and customers you *want* to work with.

> **Paul Fernandez,** Co-Founder and CEO,
> The Growth Guys

A page-turner like no other. This succinct and impactful book flips the tired concept of the customer avatar on its head and kicks it into touch. Many of the insightful lessons seem obvious in hindsight – but that is a testament to Chet's ability to dissect the complexities of value-driven behaviour and present them in meaningful, practical, and applicable ways. I now feel equipped to attract clients I can serve at the highest level through work that gives me boundless energy, lifelong fulfilment and a more profitable business.

> **Dr Steve Day,** BSc Hons BMBS. Business
> Coach, Founder of Systems and Outsourcing

I loved Chet's first book *Work Worth Doing*, so I was delighted when I heard about his second offering – *The Right Clients*. This book is packed full of insightful and accessible advice, written by someone who gets it and has been on the journey themselves. The writing itself is wonderful – it sang to my brain.

It gave me a deep sense of knowing who The Right Clients are for me, and that clarity from within has created a new energy for growing my business. Whether you've been in business a few months or a few decades, this practical guide will help you find the niche and the people that truly value your work. A great read for all coaches and entrepreneurs navigating this complex world.

Beth Stallwood, Leadership and Life Coach, Founder of Create WorkJoy

This book is a little gem. Chet has created a beautiful balance between an insightful read and a useful, practical guide. It made me stop, evaluate, look inward and ask the right questions about The Right Clients. The book takes you on a journey to find out who is important, to learn how to focus on them, and to understand how this impacts your business and your life. Chet's words give you permission to trust in yourself to make difficult decisions, and carry them out with purpose and ease, so both you and your business can flourish. *The Right Clients* is relatable, individual, and invaluable for business owners who want to show up authentic, happy and strong for their people – the right people.

Suzanne Keatley, Women's Coach and Mentor, Founder of Fitology Hub

Chet's words are grounding and stabilising. They give you permission to finally relax into doing your authentic work for your authentic people. His insightful and powerful perspective on finding The Right Clients (and having them find you) shifts away from the usual rhetoric of business guidance, and towards something you can really sink your teeth into. This book connects on so many levels, bringing to full awareness the huge impact that our clients have on our lives, and the potential we have to impact the right people. Spend time with Chet's questions. Let them seep and sink into your current beliefs. Return to the scenarios he provides. Use his guides to mould your confidence and purpose. And discover for yourself that who you serve best will also serve you best.

> **Elizabeth Brown,** Personal Development Coach, MindBodyLife Coaching

I immediately felt like I was in safe hands reading *The Right Clients*. Chet's words are filled with the confidence and camaraderie of a trusted guide; inviting us into new perspectives and motivating us towards meaningful change. Through his playful and thought-provoking writing approach, Chet dissolves industry myths and reconnects us to vision and potential in our business and in our life.

The Right Clients is as supportive as it is challenging, and as illuminating as it is pragmatic. Chet skilfully reminds us of what we already know and lets us in on the lessons that only he could know given his industry experience and unique insight. He shares with generosity, honesty and lucidity. Often, I found myself smiling in appreciation of his creative use of language, in being seen and understood, and in several moments of surprise. The energy and momentum build as Chet navigates us through this new terrain towards a rousing call to action, promising a new kind of working and a new kind of living. Affirming, disruptive and liberating, on finishing *The Right Clients* I feel reenergised, inspired and ready for more.

> **Ruth Coates MBACP,** Psychotherapist and Therapeutic Writing Guide, Founder of Writing Unbound

THE
RIGHT
CLIENTS

CHOOSE WHO YOU WORK WITH, RECLAIM YOUR ENERGY AND LEAD WITH AUTHENTICITY

CHET MORJARIA

R^ethink

First published in Great Britain in 2021 by Rethink Press
(www.rethinkpress.com)

Cover image © Shutterstock | Alex Pin

Illustrations by Jon Jacks

Disclaimer

This book is not intended to provide personalised legal, financial, or investment advice. The Author and the Publisher specifically disclaim any liability, loss or risk which is incurred as a consequence, directly or indirectly, of the use and application of any contents of this work.

For my wife, Jules – my right person

Contents

The Right Clients: An Introduction   1

The Right Clients: A Manifesto   3

ONE: The Right Reasons   7

The Right People   9

We Reflect Our People   11

Your Best Future Clients   13

Hold Nothing Back   16

The Wrong Clients   18

Full Of Fulfilment   19

Wrong And Right   21

The More You Give   23

The Wrong Signs   25

Nothing Is Unlimited   27

The Ironies Of Boundaries   29

The Mathematics Of People   30

Path To The Future   32

The Customer Is Not Always Right   34

Why Niching Is Necessary   36

Client Needs   39

Stand Up, Stand Out   41

To Be You   43

Say Yes Less   44

TWO: The Right Questions   47

Make Sense Of It All   49

Your Best Clients: T1s   51

The Core Concerns Of Your T1s   55

Their Devotion   57

Their Struggle   58

Their Desire   60

Their Perspective   62

Their Secret   64

Their Predicament   65

Your Worst Clients: T3s   67

Spot The Signs   69

Set Them Free   71

The Rest of Your Clients: T2s   73

Disproportionate Impact   76

You Already Know   78

Red Flags And Green Flags   79

No Idiot Policy   82

Rules For The Right Clients   84

Who You Spend The Most Time On   86

THREE: The Right Decisions   89

Choose Yourself   91

It's Your Choice   93

Nothing Is Forever   95

Life On Your Terms   96

The Edges Of Ourselves	97
A Life Without Boundaries	99
Commitment Without Commitments	101
Loyalty Is Misleading	102
When The Chips Are Down	104
The Right Feedback	107
Know Your Nos	109
The Meaning Of No	112
The Ability To Pay	113
They Need Help	115
Help Yourself	117
Who Needs You Now	119
Stay On The Wagon	121
The Answers Don't Change	124
Help Everyone, Help No One	125
Align Your Decisions	128
Create The Right Thing	130
The Starving Artist	132
The Bad, The Good, The Great	135
The Right Spot	136
Create The Clients	138
Meaningful Marketing	140
Why Your People Aren't Buying	142
Discounting Is Dangerous	145
Make A Difference	147
You Get What You Give	150

FOUR: The Right Support

FOUR: The Right Support 153

The Right Thing 155

The Right Support 157

The Right Challenge 160

The Right Resources 164

Acknowledgements 165

The Illustrator 169

The Author 171

The Right Clients:
An Introduction

It's not about more clients.
It's about more of The Right Clients.

We reflect who we work with,
and who we work with reflects us.

This doesn't mean passing judgement
on our people as humans.

It just means the right humans are The Right Clients.

And The Right Clients are the right humans.

It means we share the same values.
It means we do work of value for them.
It means we feel valued by them.
It means we are valuable to them.
And they are valuable to us.

You need to be right for your clients.
And your clients need to be right for you.

The Right Clients:
A Manifesto

◎ It's not about more clients.
   It's about more of The Right Clients.

◎ If they are not The Right Clients,
   then they are the wrong clients.

◎ The more you give to the wrong clients,
   the less you can give to The Right Clients.

◎ It's better to have a few of The Right Clients
   than a lot of the wrong clients.

◎ With The Right Clients, everything works.
   With the wrong clients, everything gets worse.

- ◎ Saying no to the wrong clients at the door
  isn't wrong. It's your right.

- ◎ Just because someone can pay you,
  doesn't mean they are The Right Client for you.

- ◎ A meaningful life without boundaries
  comes from a life with meaningful boundaries.

- ◎ If you can't imagine working with a client for life,
  don't spend your life working with that client.

- ◎ We reflect who we work with,
  and who we work with reflects us.

- ◎ You don't choose your niche,
  your niche chooses you.

- ◎ The quickest way to understand clients' needs
  is to understand that they are a
  previous version of you.

- ◎ Your best current clients are past versions of you.
  And your best future clients are
  present versions of you.

- ◎ The thing that is stopping them from
  embracing the support they need
  is the thing they need support with.

- ◎ The thing you need most help with
  is the thing you help others with most.

◎ It's because you haven't got it all figured out,
not despite that you haven't figured it all out,
that you can powerfully help your clients.

◎ You only need to be two levels
ahead of your clients.
You need to be only two levels
ahead of your clients.

◎ When you create for The Right Clients,
you create the right thing.
When you create for the wrong clients,
you create the wrong thing.

◎ Your marketing should compel The Right Clients
and repel the wrong clients.

◎ How much we give to our clients is not the problem.
How much we give to the wrong clients is.

ONE

The Right
Reasons

The Right
People

The Right Clients are the right people.
The right people are The Right Clients.

The right people:
 are the people who need you the most,
 are the people who you help the most,
 are the people who need your help the most.

You can decide who you work with, but first,
you need to discover who you work best with –
and understand that who you work best with,
is not the same as who you work most with.

This book is about how to understand what your
best clients look like. If you don't have any clients yet,
don't worry. Whenever you see the word 'client', just
replace it with the word 'human', and work through
these questions thinking of the people in your life.

To get you started, consider:

◎ Who have you helped powerfully in the past?

◎ Who have you helped make a big change in their lives?

◎ Who comes to you for help naturally?

◎ Who keeps coming to you for help?

◎ Who tells their friends about how much you've helped them?

We Reflect Our People

◎ We reflect who we work with,
and who we work with reflects us.

◎ We reflect who we work with.
We meet ourselves in them.
We help ourselves in them.

◎ We reflect who we work with.
We see our past self in them.
We see our true self in them.

◎ We reflect who we work with.
We absorb their energy.
We reflect their energy.

◎ Who we work with reflects us.
They are a reflection of our values.
They are a reflection of our vision.

◎ Who we work with reflects us.
They are a reflection of our work.
They are a reflection of our words.

◎ Who we work with reflects us.
They are a reflection of our efficacy.
They are a reflection of our ability.

◎ We reflect who we work with,
and who we work with reflects us.

Your Best
Future Clients

Who knows what your best future clients are thinking and feeling better than anyone?

Your best clients.

Because your best clients are present versions of your best future clients.

This means that they not only know what your best future clients are thinking and feeling right now, but they also know how your best future clients will think and feel after becoming a client and throughout their client journey.

You just need to ask your best clients the right questions to take them back to the moment they chose to make a change in their lives.

Ask your best clients:

- ◎ What helped you to realise you needed to make a change in your life?

- ◎ What helped you to understand what that change was truly about?

- ◎ What helped you to see a clear path forward?

- ◎ What helped you to trust that this was the path for you?

- ◎ What helped you to embrace the decision to get started?

- ◎ What helped you to stay on the right track?

The answers to these questions will help you to support your best future clients powerfully throughout their client journey.

Hold Nothing Back

You already give more than your means. But why doesn't it seem to be enough, no matter how much you give? Why are you not swimming in success? It's not because of your lack of trying or willing. You throw everything at helping people. But it never seems to lead to the money, time and fulfilment you spend your life working towards.

The truth is hard to swallow: it's because your lead offering doesn't hold up. And that's holding up your success. You are holding back in your lead offering – not through a lack of trying, but through a lack of understanding. You are seemingly holding nothing back, but your lack of understanding is holding everything back.

Your lead offering doesn't hold up because it wasn't built specifically for The Right Clients, so it includes a bit of everything. You want clients to stay and be happy, so you throw everything at them. And that takes everything out of you.

If you want to break free from this, you need to understand who you can help best. It's time to focus your attention on The Right Clients. Your work will become focused and powerful.

You'll truly be able to hold nothing back, in a way that is meaningful, sustainable and progressive. You will feel like you are giving the world to your clients, because now, you are.

The Wrong
Clients

If, right now, a person is not The Right Client for you,
then you're not the right coach for them.

If, right now, what they need help with most
is not how you help people most,
then you're not the right help for them.

If they are not The Right Client for you,
then they are the wrong client for you.

This doesn't mean:

- ◎ That they are bad humans.
  That you're a bad human.

- ◎ That they have done anything wrong.
  That you've done anything wrong.

- ◎ That they always were the wrong client.
  That they always will be the wrong client.

It's not wrong of you to identify that some people
are simply the wrong clients for you.

Full **Of** Fulfilment

When your business is filled with the wrong clients, you'll feel stretched thin.

Because:

◎ They want different things.

◎ Nothing is ever enough.

◎ They are always looking to take more and give less.

You're not the right coach for them, and they are not The Right Client for you.

When your business is filled with the right people, you'll feel fulfilled.

Because:

◎ You'll find they need the same thing.

◎ They can't thank you enough.

◎ They are always looking to give more, and give back.

You're the right coach for them, and they are The Right Client for you.

Wrong And Right

- The wrong clients believe they are right.
  The Right Clients believe you are right for them.

- The wrong clients debate with you.
  The Right Clients relate to you.

- The wrong clients seek the best price.
  The Right Clients seek a fair price.

- The wrong clients pay you late.
  The Right Clients pay you straight.

- The wrong clients seek the next thing.
  The Right Clients seek the right thing.

- The wrong clients give it a go.
  The Right Clients give it their all.

- The wrong clients come and go.
  The Right Clients come and stay.

- The wrong clients challenge your every move.
  The Right Clients champion your every move.

- The wrong clients want what's best for them.
  The Right Clients want what's best for all.

◎ The wrong clients drain you.
   The Right Clients fuel you.

◎ The wrong clients exhaust you.
   The Right Clients exhilarate you.

The **More**
You Give

The more you give to The Right Clients:

◎ The more they take note.

◎ The more they take action.

◎ The more they take opportunities.

◎ The more they take responsibility.

◎ The more they take off.

Whereas the more you give to the wrong clients:

◎ The more they take.

◎ The more they take the p***.

◎ The more they take advantage.

◎ The more they take exception.

◎ The more they take for granted.

The Wrong Signs

For kind, intuitive people, it can be hard to define – and trust – when you're working with the wrong clients.

Look for these signs in how you feel when you're working with the wrong clients:

- You feel you can't do your best work.
  You feel you're not setting the best example.

- You feel you're not being true to yourself.
  You feel you're not being true to your client.

- You feel you're beginning to resent the work.
  You feel you're beginning to resent the client.

- You feel a negative impact on your mental health.
  You feel a negative impact on your physical health.

- You feel a negative impact on your relationship with yourself.
  You feel a negative impact on your relationship with others.

- You feel a negative impact on your work with the client.
  You feel a negative impact on your work with other clients.

Trust yourself to trust these signs.

The right people fill your cup.
The wrong people empty your cup.

If the balance between the wrong and The Right Clients tips the wrong way, your cup will get emptier and emptier, which often manifests as frustration, overwhelm, guilt and self-doubt. This means you are not able to serve The Right Clients as powerfully as you would like, or as meaningfully as they deserve.

The only way to tip that balance is to set the wrong people free and create space for more of The Right Clients.

Fill your cup with conviction, focus and purpose.

Nothing Is
Unlimited

Nothing is unlimited:

◎ Our time.

◎ Our attention.

◎ Our money.

◎ Our energy.

These determine our ability to:

◎ Make decisions meaningfully.

◎ Serve our people powerfully.

◎ Lead a meaningful community.

It is only when we consider that:

◎ Every person is an opportunity.

◎ Every opportunity has a cost.

◎ Every person also has a cost.

That we can weigh up each person's impact on our ability to:

- ◎ Make decisions meaningfully.

- ◎ Serve our people powerfully.

- ◎ Lead a meaningful community.

Thinking like this isn't limited or limiting. It's fulfilling and freeing.

A business and life without limits come from embracing our limits.

The Ironies Of Boundaries

The people who need them don't end up setting them.
The people who set them don't end up needing them.

Those clients who need to respect them
will ask for special treatment and abuse them.
Those clients who could abuse them
don't need to be asked to respect them.

Setting meaningful boundaries with others comes
from setting meaningful boundaries for yourself.
A meaningful life without boundaries comes
from a life with meaningful boundaries.

The Mathematics Of People

Just because your vision has you at its origin, it doesn't mean you have to be the singular coordinator.

Factor the right people into the equation:

- ◎ Those who connect with the common denominator of your vision.

- ◎ Those who are on parallel paths.

- ◎ Those who share a similar trajectory.

Then your vision becomes greater than the sum of its parts, despite our tendencies to think the inverse – that when we expand our vision through others it becomes shared and averaged between us all.

Engage fully with those people who multiply your vision.

Select wisely those people who add to your vision.

Interact sparingly with those people who divide your focus from your vision.

Ignore completely those people who take away from your vision.

When you connect with the right people, you'll feel the force of your vision exponentially increase.

Path To
The Future

As purpose-driven coaches, we can find ourselves craving more meaning in our work. Especially when our lives are full of distractions and frustrations, both personal and professional.

The last thing we feel we have time to do is take a moment to explore what drives us and our people, as well as what limits us and our people, and weave that understanding into our business and communications.

But if we are to find our way to working on our terms, never mind towards living a life on our terms, then building a business we believe in, and creating marketing that speaks to our people's souls, from the heart of our value and values, is the path to the future we desire.

The Customer Is
Not Always Right

'The customer is always right', is wrong.
The customer is not always right.

- The customer doesn't always know what's right for them.

- The customer doesn't always know what they need.

- The customer doesn't always know what they want.

When you realise the customer is not always right,
and doesn't always know what's right for them,
you realise that the right thing to do is to help them
make the right move.

- Sometimes that is to encourage them to work with you.

- Sometimes that is to discourage them from working with you.

- Sometimes that is to encourage them to work with someone else.

Business is a delicate interplay between doing the right thing by your customer and knowing that what you are doing is right.

Knowing that what you are doing is right comes from your vision, your values and your mission.

Doing the right thing by your customer comes from understanding your people, their dilemmas and their dreams.

The customer is often wrong.
The market is always right.

Why Niching
Is **Necessary**

Niching means deeply understanding who The Right Client is for you and focusing your offerings and marketing on them.

This isn't a nice-to-have. It's necessary for truly meaningful work.

If you're not niching...

... you're guessing

Despite what many business coaches say, just trying things out and seeing what lands is not a business or marketing strategy. In fact, it's a sure-fire waste of time, energy and money.

... you're competing

When you truly know who your niche is, you'll be in a market of one. The whole reason they are your niche is that no one understands them better than you, no one can help them better than you and no one can get them better results than you. They are The Right Clients for you.

... you're underperforming

Your ability to serve powerfully is a product of doing your best work with those who need it most. Those who need it the most are your niche. Unless you're working with these clients, you're working below your true potential and you'll always feel that something is missing.

... you're undercharging

You'll only be able to charge what you're truly worth when you work with those who truly value your work and you. Without understanding your true niche you'll always feel, 'I can't charge any more' – and you'll be right.

... you're overcompensating

Your desire to overdeliver and your hunch that your people aren't happy will push you to overcompensate by giving more and more and more. But this will yield diminishing returns at best, because unless you're working with your niche, your people will never be truly happy with your work.

... you're fighting

◎ Against the market.

◎ Against your competitors.

◎ Against your clients.

◎ Against your work.

◎ Against yourself.

Enough of the fighting,
It's time to get niching.

Client Needs

Often, clients don't know what they need.
Half the time, they barely know what they want.

The quickest way to understand client needs
is to understand that your clients are a previous
version of you.

Your clients' needs are the same as your needs.
They need what you need.
You need what they need.

Clients need to feel listened to, understood
and respected.

If your marketing and sales don't do that,
you need to adapt.

Your clients' needs are not as individual
as you might think.
There are common denominators
and linked limiters.

Avatars don't cut it when it comes to
understanding clients.
They are baseless, impractical
and one-dimensional.

But your clients' needs are only
one half of the equation.
Your ability to serve those needs meaningfully
is the other half.

The entire success of your business model
is predicated on aligning these two halves.

Stand Up, Stand Out

When you know what you stand for and what you stand against – in other words, your vision, values and vocation – you can stand up for your beliefs, without being stand-offish.

When you know who you stand with and who you can't stand – in other words, who The Right Clients are for you – you can take a stand on who you choose to work with.

When you know how you stand out and how you stand apart – in other words, how you do your best work – you can stand your competition aside and stand the industry on its head.

You'll be able to:

◎ Stand firm in your choices.

◎ Stand out in your industry.

◎ Stand tall in your positioning.

◎ Stand alone in your market.

◎ Stand apart in your marketing.

You'll be able to set up your stand
in a way that stands the test of time.

To Be You

It's true that clients want to do what you do.

And that clients want to have what you have.

But it's when you see that your clients want to be
like you – and even that your clients want to *be* you –
that you can own who you are to them and what
you do for them.

Say Yes Less

When we start out with work, we're taught to take opportunities. To welcome possibility and to embrace probabilities. In short, to say yes more. We test and try. We engage and explore. We mess up and make mistakes. We live and learn. We are headstrong. And we make headway.

Saying yes more seems to be a gateway to the life we desire. We carry that on and forward. It becomes a default. A pattern so ingrained that we say yes, even when we mean no. We miss the fact that along the way we have gathered experience and experiences that can help us decipher and decide which opportunities are worthwhile and which are worthless. Which are worth pursuing. Which are worth refusing. Which are worth parking.

Let's call it instinct. Instinct is the result of our experience and experiences, and our values and vision, all wrapped up in a moment of decision. But instead of backing ourselves, we back ourselves into a corner and take on work that doesn't suit us or serve us. The problem is, the more work we do where we are less than our best, the more we feel lost and the more we feel stressed.

We want to be of service to our people. But we think that comes from saying yes more, when actually it comes from saying yes less. Because saying yes less to all people leaves more space to say yes more to the right people. It's when we say yes more to the right people that we give ourselves the opportunity to help those who need us the most with the work that we do best.

It might feel counterintuitive, but next time it feels instinctive, say yes less and say no more. In doing so, you'll say no to the imposter monster and to the distraction, exhaustion and frustration that comes from expectations we can never meet.

Instead, you'll find yourself valuing your time, your worth and your abilities.

It's when you find yourself here that The Right Clients will find you.

TWO

The
Right
Questions

Make Sense
Of It All

Before The Right Clients can understand you, you need to understand The Right Clients.

Humans make sense of the world through the senses. In order for us to understand humans – in this case our clients – the senses are the perfect place to start.

Here are three sets of questions to help you understand The Right Clients.

What do they see?

◎ What do they see in the marketplace?

◎ What are they watching and reading?

◎ What do they see in their surroundings?

What do they hear?

◎ What are they hearing from those closest to them?

◎ What are they hearing from the media?

◎ What and who are they listening to?

What do they feel?

- ◎ What are their desires?

- ◎ What are their struggles?

- ◎ What are their secrets?

If your clients truly understand you, and feel understood by you, you no longer have just clients. You have The Right Clients. You have champions of you and your business who will spread your good work to others who see, hear and feel the same things as them.

The rest of this chapter will help you make even more sense of your clients. To understand them better, and deeper. To understand them better than they understand themselves.

Because when you are able to understand them at that level, you can speak with them at that level. That's when you can influence what they see, hear and feel.

And that's what defines what they do.

Your **Best** Clients: **T1s**

Your best clients are The Right Clients, and The Right Clients are your best clients.

We need to deeply understand who our best clients are. To do that, we need to understand what our best clients deeply need. But we can't find out these deep client needs via direct questions or surveys, because they are not conscious needs. And let's be honest, clients barely know what they want, never mind what they need. Instead, we need to profile our best clients and look for patterns in their limiters, behaviours and desires.

Before we profile our best clients, we need we need to identify them.

Use the following exercises to narrow down your three best clients. You'll then profile them in the next few chapters.

Your best clients get it.

◎ There's a human connection.

◎ You get them, they get you.

◎ They understand and champion changes.

Write down the names of three clients these statements best describe.

Your best clients are champions.

◎ They have had incredible transformations.

◎ They are your best testimonials.

◎ They are champions of you and the business.

Write down the names of three clients these statements best describe.

Your best clients teach you.

◎ You learn from them.

◎ You ask their opinion about changes.

◎ They are honest yet encouraging.

Write down the names of three clients these statements best describe.

Your best clients inspire you.

◎ They inspire you.

◎ They inspire your work.

◎ They inspire your other clients.

Write down the names of three clients these statements best describe.

Your best clients fuel you.

◎ They give you energy.

◎ They give you conviction.

◎ They give you confidence.

Write down the names of three clients these statements best describe.

Your best clients respect you.

◎ They respect your work.

◎ They respect your support.

◎ They respect your time.

Write down the names of three clients these statements best describe.

Which three names come up again and again?

Let's call these your Tier 1 (T1) clients. These are your best clients. These are The Right Clients.

The concept of meaningful business is ultimately simple:

1. Identify and understand your T1 clients.

2. Model your business on them.

3. Go and get more of them.

The Core Concerns Of Your T1s

Avatars are ancient.
Demographics are one-dimensional.

Humans are complex.
Humans are emotional.

We need more than a set of demographics and data points to understand the depth, dimensions and decisions of our people.

There are six core concerns of our best people, our T1s, that we need to explore to truly get under their skin and to know them better than they know themselves. These are:

1. Their devotion.

2. Their struggle.

3. Their desire.

4. Their perspective.

5. Their secret.

6. Their predicament.

It's when we're at this level of understanding that we can:

◎ Speak to their deepest needs and desires.

◎ Speak to their showstoppers and limiters.

◎ Impact and influence their decisions
and direction.

◎ Lead them towards a mutually fulfilling outcome.

Use the explanations, descriptions, statements and
prompts in this section to help you deeply understand
your people. Remember that one of the best examples
of your best people, your T1s, is yourself.

Their Devotion

Our devotions can be dangerous. They can become our overriding obsessions. They can become our just-do-it defaults.

Although these devotions might not be bad things (for example, a devotion to helping everyone, caring for everyone, doing everything, or questioning everything), too much of a good thing can become a bad thing.

But because these are meaningful, honourable, humble devotions, we do them without realising, until they become our undoing.

Answer these questions to understand the devotion of your T1s:

◎ Who or what are they devoted to in life?

◎ What is their life more-than-full of?

◎ Who can they not help but help?

Then use one of these prompts to frame the devotion of your T1s:

◎ You're the type of person who...

◎ You can't help but...

◎ It's instinctive for you to...

Their **Struggle**

Every coin has two sides. Every benefit has a cost. Every deed has a consequence.

We don't always realise the impact of what we are doing for others, on ourselves. We don't always consider the personal effect of our actions, habits, and cycles. We get used to the expectations and the limitations. We become accustomed to the discomforts and the disconnection.

We don't always see the cracks when they start to appear. And we don't always want to acknowledge them, never mind share them.

Answer these questions to understand the struggle of your T1s:

◎   What are the individual consequences of their devotion?

◎   What is the inevitable flip side of their devotion?

◎   What is the secret struggle that comes with their devotion?

Then use one of these prompts to frame the struggle of your T1s:

◎ You find yourself...

◎ This leaves you...

◎ You do so without...

Their Desire

When we accept our struggles,
we start to accept our truth.

When we accept our truth,
we start to wonder if there's anything else.

When we wonder if there's anything else,
we see that there may be another way.

When we see that there is another way,
we start to believe our future could look different.

When we believe our future could look different,
we begin to explore it.

When we explore it,
we begin to seek it.

When we see it,
we begin to crave it.

It takes acceptance of our struggle
to see a different future.

It takes embracing our struggle
to step into that future.

Answer these questions to understand the desire of your T1s:

◎ Where do they yearn for a different path?

◎ What do they seek?

◎ What do they crave in their future?

Then use one of these prompts to frame the desire of your T1s:

◎ You're left wondering...

◎ You seek...

◎ You enjoy exploring...

Their **Perspective**

Our approach to life is often created:
from our need to be accepted,
from our need to be needed,
from our need to be connected.

We find ourselves living life in line:
with how we think we need to be,
with what we think we need to do,
with what we think we should do.

We strive to be the person:
that we need to be,
that we're told to be,
that we think we should be.

This is a motivator.
But also, a manipulator.

Answer these questions to understand the
perspective of your T1s:

◎   How do they approach their life?

◎   How do they approach their work?

◎   How do they approach their communities?

Then use one of these prompts to frame the perspective of your T1s:

◎ You approach life...

◎ You find yourself...

◎ You strive to...

Their Secret

Our ambitions and intentions, while well-intentioned, come with secret doubts, shameful guilt and serious overwhelm.

They are difficult to deal with at the best of times. But if we're to be our best selves, and at our best for others, we need to understand who we are at the worst of times.

Until we tell the truth to ourselves about these emotions, we'll never be able to be true to our intentions and truly transcend our ambitions.

Answer these questions to understand the secret of your T1s:

◎   What do they doubt about themselves?

◎   What do they feel guilty about?

◎   What do they feel overwhelmed by?

Then use one of these prompts to frame the secret of your T1s:

◎   But you're not sure if...

◎   If you dare admit it...

◎   But truth be told, you're...

Their **Predicament**

If we don't acknowledge, accept and embrace emotions, they can bubble up and boil over – and spoil our plans, scupper us, sabotage us, make us sabotage ourselves, or even make us sabotage others.

We find ourselves in places we don't want to be, doing things we don't want to do, or not doing things we want to do.

Our positive actions, abilities and ambitions can run into negative reactions, predicaments and temptations.

Answer these questions to understand the predicament of your T1s:

◎   What impact do their emotions have on them?

◎   What impact do their emotions have on those closest to them?

◎   How do these emotions stop them from taking action?

Then use one of these prompts to frame the predicament of your T1s:

- ◎ You somehow end up...

- ◎ This affects your...

- ◎ It's tempting to...

Your **Worst** Clients: **T3s**

These are the clients you secretly dread.
Although you may barely admit that to yourself.

These are the clients who give you weird
negative feelings.
Although you're not quite sure why.

These are the clients who take up far too much
of your headspace.
Although you try hard to not let that happen.

These are the clients you give a lot to.
Although you don't get much from them.

These are the clients you feel you're fighting against.
Although strangely, you also fight for them.

These are the clients who pay you the least money.
Although they give you the most hassle.

These are the clients who hold you back.
Although you may not realise it.

These are the clients you'd drop if you could.
Although you'd still feel bad about it.

The first step in dealing with your T3s is to objectively work through the above statements and write down the clients that come to mind. These are your worst clients, the wrong clients, your T3s.

The second step is to look over that list and understand that writing it doesn't make you a bad human.

The third step is to set these clients free from your business, to make space for those who need you, value you and respect you more than they do.

Spot **The** Signs

By the time a T3 client becomes a real problem, it's too late.

The classic signs of a T3 are:

◎ They no longer function.

◎ They are causing friction.

◎ They have formed a faction.

Let's break that down.

They no longer function.

◎ They are turning up less to group or team sessions.

◎ They are showing up less in group or team sessions.

◎ They are not responding to communication.

◎ Their timekeeping has slackened.

◎ Their energy has lessened.

They are causing friction.

◎ They have influenced other clients negatively.

◎ They have caused conflict within your client base.

◎ They have caused conflict within your team.

◎ They have taken up too much of your time and energy.

◎ They have taken up too much of your head space and sanity.

They have formed a faction.

◎ They are less of a team player.

◎ They have created a small subgroup.

◎ They turn their back to you.

◎ They try and turn others away from you.

◎ They set up against you.

You need to be able to spot the signs before they take over your thoughts, take over your people and take over your business.

Set Them Free

When you recognise the wrong client, a T3, set them free.

Tightening your grip, or cracking the whip, in the hope that things flip, will only create a further dip.

And leaving them be doesn't help to set you free.

This situation will only slip, until you decide to make the snip.

It's time to say what both of you have needed to say.

See this as an opportunity to clear up ambiguity.

Do it swiftly and decisively, with respect and honesty.

Do it with dignity for the past, and finality for the future.

Do it with care for who they are, yet honesty about what they do.

Do it with boundaries for you, and with limits for them.

Do it as the right decision for you, and the right choice for them.

Do it with as much love on the way out as you showed them on the way in.

When you set them free, you set yourself free.
And you'll be able to envision a future you didn't
know you couldn't see.

Open your eyes. Set them free.

The Rest of Your Clients: T2s

Your T2 clients are probably the majority of your clients and the majority of your income.

They are neither your best clients, nor your worst. They are not the easiest to work with, nor the most difficult.

They are your bread and butter.
They are your in and out.
They are your up and down.
They are your 'middle of the road'.
They are your 'straight down the line'.

You can help them, which is part of the problem. You can probably help them better than anyone else you know.

The work is straightforward.
The work is unexceptional.

They don't light your fire.
And they don't fire you up.

They don't champion you.
And you don't champion them.

Perhaps the most important distinction to make when it comes to defining your T2 clients is that although these aren't your worst clients, they are not your best clients either.

And while a business full of T2s – those who need you, but not as much as others; those you can help, but not as much as you can help others – has a chance of being 'successful', this is not the ultimate goal.

The problem with T2s, is that your work with them expands to fill your available time.

You run around trying to keep them happy.

You put resources into ideas that never quite seem to hit the mark.

You serve them, but not at your best.
You end up always fighting against yourself.
You end up always feeling you can do more.
And you never quite find that feeling of fulfilment.

Until you have a business full of T1s – those who need you more than any others, those you can help more than any others, those who fuel you, inspire you, get you, and champion you – there is little chance of building a fulfilling business.

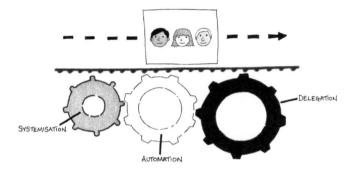

When you have a business full of T1s, a little input from you goes a long way. Which gives you the time, inspiration and vision for refining your understanding of how you do what you do best, using this to serve the specific needs of your T1s as powerfully as possible, and shaping your world to do as much of this as you can.

In the meantime, box off the energy that you spend with T2s, and use systemisation, automation and delegation to keep it that way.

Disproportionate Impact

Your T1s are those clients who you help just by doing what you do. The work comes almost too easily to you, but it has huge impact on them. Your help is disproportionate to the impact you deliver, in a good way.

Your T2s are those clients who you help through the mechanics of what you do. But it takes work and time. It helps them, but in equal proportion to your endeavour. Your help is proportionate to the impact you deliver. They get out what you put in.

Your T3s are those clients who you help on the fringes of what you do. The work is difficult and complex and doesn't seem to have much impact on them. Your help is disproportionate to the impact you deliver, in a bad way.

If you want to impact The Right Clients in the right way – and make the most impact, with the least resource – then look for positive disproportionate impact in the clients that you serve and the work that you do.

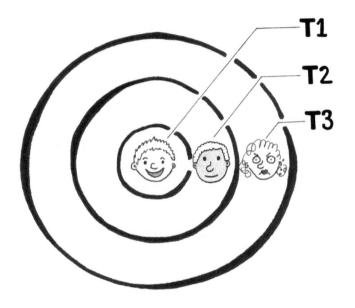

T1

T2

T3

You Already Know

You already know who your next problem clients are.
They are not going to appear out of the blue.
They won't suddenly be ready to leave.
They are already in your sights.
They are already disengaged from your work.
They are already sending you signals.
Are you seeing them, or ignoring them?

You already know who your next top clients are.
They are not going to appear out of the blue.
They won't suddenly be ready to buy.
They are already in your sights.
They are already engaging with your work.
They are already sending you signals.
Are you seeing them, or ignoring them?

Red Flags And Green Flags

How do we identify our T1s and T3s long before they become clients?

If we can do so, we'll save ourselves time and energy. If we can't, we'll run headlong into headaches.

Have you ever taken T3 clients on board who, in retrospect, showed early warning signs? Those are their red flags.

Have you ever noticed that T1 clients seem to approach your initial interactions in the same way? Those are their green flags.

Both types of flags are planted firmly in values.

T1s share your values.

◎   What's important to them is important to you.

◎   What's important to you is important to them.

The opposite is true of T3s.

- What's important to them is important to them.
- What's important to you is not important to them.

For example, your values might be:

- Responsibility.
- Respect.
- Challenge.

Ask yourself: what do these values look like in T1 clients? This could be:

- Responsibility: sending over prep work before coaching calls.
- Respect: being respectful of your time and your boundaries.
- Challenge: saying 'I'm ready to be challenged' and being open to fresh perspectives.

Then ask yourself: what do these values look like in T3 clients? This could be:

- Lack of personal responsibility: undertaking multiple concurrent similar pieces of professional development.

- ◎ Lack of respect: not replying or responding, or taking days.

- ◎ Not open to challenge: saying 'I've done the coaching thing' and not being open to alternative perspectives.

A side note – don't mistake a red herring for a red flag. For example, missing a meeting, but communicating this to you with respect and responsibility. This probably isn't a red flag, just a red herring.

Determine the green flags and red flags of your people, and you'll save yourself a lot of time and energy when choosing who to work with. This means more time and energy to spend on the work that matters and the people who matter.

No Idiot **Policy**

Many business owners declare they have a 'no idiot policy'.

That's something to respect.

- ◎ Respect for choosing who they work with.

- ◎ Respect for protecting their business and clients.

- ◎ Respect for conserving their energy and headspace.

But 'no idiots' isn't the ultimate goal. It's the starting point. Not allowing the wrong people into the business is not the same as only allowing the right people into the business.

It's the same as when a business owner says, 'I'm really lucky none of my clients are awful.' But that's not a matter of luck – or it shouldn't be. It's a matter of choice. It's not enough just to have no T3 clients. Life and business is about more than that.

If you want to build a Business With Meaning – a business that is aligned with your true values, gives your clients deep value, and takes you toward being emotionally and financially valued – that can only be done when you know who the right people are and you actively bring them into the business.

Not allowing T3s into the business is a starting point. But it's when you only allow T1s in that you'll hit the turning point you're seeking.

When you fill a business with the wrong people, nothing works.

But when you fill a business with the right people, everything works.

Rules For The **Right** Clients

The right humans are The Right Clients.
The Right Clients are the right humans.

For those clients you're unsure about, ask yourself
these questions to determine your position on
working with them:

- ◎ Do you feel an instant connection?

- ◎ Do they fill you with conviction?

- ◎ Could you work with them for life?

- ◎ Could you live with them for work?

- ◎ Would you introduce them to your family?

- ◎ Would you go on holiday with them?

- ◎ Can you see your values in their actions?

- ◎ Can you see your previous self in their journey?

If you answer yes to all of these, there's something there. Trust your instincts. Let them in.

If you answer no to most of these, there's something missing. Trust your instincts. Let them go free.

Who You Spend The Most Time On

It has been said that we are the average of the five people we spend the most time with. That includes the five people we spend the most time *on*.

Fill your books with T1 clients and your team with T1 humans who are committed to the business and each other, and you'll find yourself spending more and more time with people who fuel your fire.

Spend a large proportion of your time on T3s, troublesome clients and disruptive team members (including business partners) and, before you know it, you'll be spending more time on them than those who are truly and deeply important to you.

You are the average of the five people you spend the most time on. It's time to ask yourself:

◎   Who do you want to be?

◎   Who do you not want to be?

Realign your time with your values.

THREE

The
Right
Decisions

Choose Yourself

Marketeers talk about getting people to 'know, like and trust' you, so that when the time comes, they choose you. This can create a feeling of eternally waiting to be chosen.

Waiting for people to choose to work with you. Waiting for people to choose to pay you money. Waiting for people to choose to stay with you.

But it's not about you being chosen. If you think like that, you're already screwed.

It's not about them, it's about you.

It's not about them choosing you, it's about you choosing you.

For people to choose you, you've got to choose yourself.

For people to know you, you've got to know yourself.

For people to like you, you've got to like yourself.

For people to trust you, you've got to trust yourself.

Stop waiting to be chosen.
Start choosing yourself.

It's **Your Choice**

Instead of asking how to find more people who want to work with you, ask yourself how to choose the people you want to work with.

This creates a powerful shift in the energy you put out into the world. Humans are astute. Especially your type of humans. They pick up on cues in your communication. If you're thinking, 'I really, really hope more people will want to work with me', this comes through in your marketing, whether you intend it or not.

And you'll end up working with the wrong clients. People who you can't work in your zone with. This means they won't see your true value and you will be constantly trying to make them happy. No one wins.

If you're thinking, 'I decide who gets to work with me', this means you can choose to do your best work with the people who need it the most.

And here's how that plays out:

Stage 1
You choose yourself.

Stage 2

You stop just working with anyone and everyone who chooses you.

Stage 3

You start choosing who you work with.

Stage 4

You just work with those who you have chosen.

It starts with deciding that who you spend time on is your choice.

Nothing Is Forever

Nothing is forever.

Getting it right means making the right decision.
The decision to set ourselves free from whoever and
whatever no longer serves us, right here and right now.

Nothing is forever.

Getting it right means making the right decision for now.
The decision to own who and what serves us, right
here and right now.

Nothing is forever.

All we know is the truth for now.
All we can do is make the right decision for now.

Life On Your Terms

There's a myth that a life (and business) on your terms has to be at the expense of everyone else, a 'my way or the highway' state of affairs. The truth is entirely the opposite.

Setting boundaries when it comes to time and money allows you to focus on the people who really matter, both from a personal and a client perspective.

It also allows you to focus on the work that matters. It allows you to have even more powerful interactions with your clients, because the elephant in the room is no longer there looming over you.

Before you make this shift in business, you need to make this shift in yourself. It's a transition from living life based on the demands and expectations of others, towards a life that is lived on your terms. It's on you to decide that you're no longer standing for that – and that it's time to focus on who and what are important to you.

The Edges Of
Ourselves

Setting boundaries with clients can feel awkward and aggressive. It can feel formal and fussy. It can feel exclusionary and elitist.

Let's reshape boundaries together.
And let's make them about 'together'.

What if we apply an intention of value and values when setting boundaries with clients, instead of an intention of instruction and regulation?

What if instead of being about commitments to each other, our boundaries were about commitment to each other?

What if setting boundaries was less about setting exclusions, and more about setting expectations?

What if instead of treating boundaries as rules, we treated boundaries as roles?

What if instead of using boundaries as guardrails, we used boundaries as handrails?

What if instead of seeing boundaries as 'Don't cross this line', we saw boundaries as 'This is our space'?

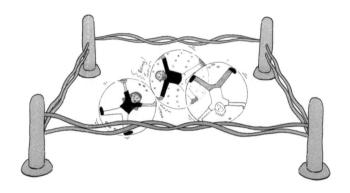

What if our boundaries were less about rounding the edges of our clients' behaviour, and more about finding the edges of our own behaviours?

When it comes down to the wire, boundaries are less about protecting us from clients, and more about protecting us from ourselves.

A Life Without Boundaries

It can feel like setting boundaries is the wrong thing
to do. And until we align with why setting boundaries
is the right thing to do, both for ourselves *and* others,
we won't be able to do it meaningfully.

Living a life without boundaries comes from
setting clear, meaningful boundaries. This means
boundaries that create a bond between you and
your people, rather than a block.

Here are some ideas you may want to consider
when it comes to setting meaningful boundaries:

Setting meaningful boundaries doesn't harm our
relationships with others.
Setting meaningful boundaries helps our
relationships with others.

Setting meaningful boundaries doesn't mean
letting people down.
Setting meaningful boundaries means letting
things go.

Setting meaningful boundaries doesn't mean creating strict rules.
Setting meaningful boundaries means creating space to explore.

Setting meaningful boundaries doesn't mean turning people away from what they need.
Setting meaningful boundaries means turning people toward what they need.

Setting meaningful boundaries doesn't mean a lack of respect for others.
Setting meaningful boundaries means total respect for others and yourself.

Setting meaningful boundaries doesn't mean a lack of responsibility toward others.
Setting meaningful boundaries means total responsibility for others and yourself.

Setting meaningful boundaries doesn't take away opportunities.
Setting meaningful boundaries creates opportunities.

Setting meaningful boundaries doesn't feel bad.
Setting meaningful boundaries feels right.

Setting meaningful boundaries means helping yourself more.
But that doesn't have to mean helping others less.

Commitment
Without
Commitments

More commitment to our people doesn't have to mean more commitments to people.

The more energy you commit to the wrong clients, the less energy you can commit to The Right Clients.

Less energy on commitments to the wrong clients means more energy for commitment to The Right Clients.

This is how you create more commitment to your people without more commitments to people.

Loyalty Is Misleading

Setting free those people who once were, but are no longer The Right Clients, can be a heart-pulling, gut-wrenching decision, even when you know it needs to happen.

We often put our inability to set them free down to a guiding value of loyalty. But loyalty can be a misleading guide.

The questions to ask yourself about loyalty, are to question if loyalty is true to you.

◎ Is loyalty truly one of your values, or does loyalty not feature in your values?

◎ Are you being true to yourself here, or are you being true to who you think you should be?

I'm not saying loyalty isn't important. And I'm not saying loyalty isn't important to *you*. But is loyalty so important to you that it trumps all your other values?

I'd rather show up with my true values in my pocket:

◎ Honesty – to myself and to my clients.

◎ Respect – for myself and for my clients.

◎ Responsibility – to myself and to my clients.

These values, my values, trump everything else when it comes to making meaningful, true decisions, every time.

When The Chips Are Down

When the chips are down, we learn two big lessons:

◎ What is important to us.

◎ Who is important to us.

Let's start with what is important to us. When times are tough, we learn lessons about ourselves. We get given a strong dose of perspective. We make promises to ourselves that things need to change. In particular, we vow to make space for Work Worth Doing and The Right Clients.

On that note, let's talk about who is important to us. Notice how when times are tricky, the kind people get kinder and the best people get better. Those people are The Right Clients, and they remain right by your side the whole time. They openly show support, offer additional help, offer to pay more and ask for little in return. You couldn't be happier to have them on your side.

The lesson here is to look after your T1 clients. Nurture and engage them. Make them feel special.

Tell them your ideas first. Ask for their feedback. It's OK to 'favour' some clients. They are the reason you are still in the game.

And notice how, when times are tricky, the mean people get meaner and the worst people disappear. Business-wise, this does you a favour.

Those who are the wrong clients disappear. They are the first to exit. They take up so much time and take so much energy, but never seem to respect or appreciate it. You breathe a sigh of relief as they step out of the door.

The lesson here is not to accept those T3 clients back. It is tempting to reopen your doors to all, to 'make up' for lost business. That is a mistake and will have you saddled with headaches in no time.

When you look back on those hard times, you can apply those same principles to other people in your life, as harsh as it may seem.

◎   Who have you truly missed?

◎   Who have you connected with?

◎   Who has connected with you?

◎   Who only makes an appearance when they want or need something?

◎   Who have you been glad to have a little space from?

These things are telling.

The biggest danger when things get better is the danger of slipping back into old relationships and habits and so finding ourselves in the same life patterns, the ones we have vowed to do something about. Old habits and default behaviours will always come back to bite us if we are not conscious of and proactive in doing something different.

The biggest opportunity when things get better is to do something different, to make meaningful changes to our businesses and lives, based on who and what are deeply important to us. To consciously and actively create new behavioural patterns that will serve our people and ourselves, and lead to the lives we have promised them, and ourselves.

The Right Feedback

As the type of person who gives our whole self to our people, critical feedback can be overwhelming and consuming. We are grateful for the openness and the opportunity to learn and grow, so that we can be even better at helping our people. But at the same time, we can take critical feedback so deeply to heart that we become consumed with guilt and self-doubt.

Consider this: feedback given to you by the right people makes your relationship better, while feedback given to you by the wrong people makes your relationship worse. That's because feedback is as much a reflection of the giver as it is of the receiver – if not more so.

T3s will give you feedback with 'brutal honesty'. But brutal honesty isn't necessary. You can be honest without being brutal. How about 'respectfully honest' instead? T1s will give you feedback with respectful honesty.

T3s will give you feedback whether you ask for it or not. But it's not feedback, it's just their opinion. Feedback is more meaningful if it's ready to be received.

How about asking if it's meaningful to give feedback first? T1s will ask your permission before giving you feedback.

T3s will give you feedback expecting you to action everything. But that's up to you, not up to them. Just as it's the giver's prerogative to provide feedback, it's the receiver's prerogative to decide what to do with it – if anything.

T1s will give you feedback knowing you'll do the right thing. Which feels like:

◎ Respectful honesty.

◎ Freedom of choice.

◎ Personal responsibility.

Feedback can be valuable. But values-led feedback, from the right people, is invaluable.

Know Your Nos

Success comes from continually refining your understanding of how you do what you do best, using this to serve the specific needs of others as powerfully as possible, and shaping your world to do as much of this as you can.

Shaping your world involves continually finding a balance between two components:

◉ Saying yes to the right work with the right people.

◉ Saying no to the wrong work with the wrong people.

Saying no to the wrong work with the wrong people can be hard, because:

◉ You still find it tricky to identify the wrong people.

◉ You still find it difficult to say no to the wrong work.

You need to know your 'No' strategies. Ways of saying 'No' that feel meaningful and helpful to you, and to those people you are saying no to.

Ways of saying no that you can use when you need to say it on the spot, so that you don't stumble into saying 'Yes' by default.

Here are three 'No' strategies to get you started:

'That's a brilliant goal. I know someone who can help you with that much better than I can – try [meaningful recommendation].'

'Thanks for thinking of me. I've been refining my understanding of what I do best, and I've come to realise that I'm best at helping [The Right Clients] – so that's who I'm focusing on giving my best to, which means cutting down on all other work.'

'I'm honoured, thank you. I'm focusing on helping [The Right Clients] to the best of my ability, so sadly, I can't help you with [requested work] right now, out of respect and responsibility to them.'

None of these statements are palming things off.
None of these statements are putting things off.
All of these statements help people to understand your refined perspective and focus on the right people, and the right work.

Know your 'No' strategies.

The Meaning Of No

'No' isn't a refusal.
It's an acceptance.

'No' isn't a never.
It's a not right now.

'No' isn't a block.
It's a boundary.

'No' isn't a moment of denial.
It's a moment of truth.

'No' isn't a problem.
It's a solution.

'No' isn't an unfairness.
It's a favour.

'No' isn't irresponsible.
It's a responsibility.

'No' isn't a disservice.
It's a service.

'No' isn't a mutual loss.
It's a mutual win.

The Ability To Pay

We hear that a person's ability to pay should be a key factor in deciding that they're The Right Client for you.

That's not quite true.

A person's ability to pay is not an indicator that they are The Right Client for you. A person's ability to pay is much more of an indicator of whether your offering is right for them and whether this is the right time for them.

A person's ability to pay should never be your only deciding factor in whether someone becomes your client.

The Right Clients are those people who really *need* your help and who *you* can really help. Ability to pay is a terrible way of classifying those who need your help.

In fact, an over-eagerness to pay can be an indicator of the prospective client not having a true understanding of the depth and nature of the problem they came to you to decipher.

You might even say that a person's over-eagerness to pay is an indicator that they are the wrong client for you.

It shouldn't be a case of, 'If they can pay, they are right.' Nor should it be a case of, 'If they can't pay, they are wrong.'

If you're really in this to help people, create impact and find fulfilment, then you'll find a way to do so.

And if they really want to work with you, then they will find a way to do so.

They Need Help

'But they really need help.'

For us givers and helpers, one of the hardest parts about choosing who you work with is knowing that you can't help everyone who needs it.

Remember that not everyone who needs help needs *your* help, wants help, or is ready for help.

Not everyone who needs help, needs *your* help.
Is this where you do your best work?
Or will this pull you away from your best work?

Not everyone who needs help, wants help.
Do they want help?
Or, do you want to give them help more than they want to receive it?

Not everyone who needs help, is ready for help.
Are they in a position to embrace your help?
Or, do they have some work to do themselves first?

Focus on:

- ◎ Those who you are best placed to help.

- ◎ Those who want your help.

- ◎ Those who are ready for your help.

You'll find that that a little of your help goes a long way.

Help **Yourself**

Your best current clients are past versions of you.

So help yourself. Ask yourself the below questions. Then deliver your insights to your people.

From the perspective of what you know now, what would you tell yourself three months ago? Are you talking about this to your clients?

Think about:

◎   Your realisations.

◎   Your recent lessons.

◎   Your latest perceptions.

From the perspective of where you are now, what would you tell yourself three years ago? Are you talking about this to your prospects?

This is:

◎   Your crystal ball.

◎   Your lived experience.

◎   Your moments of meaningful change.

From the perspective of who you are now, what would you tell yourself three decades ago? Are you talking about this to the world?

This is:

◎ Your origin story.

◎ Your personal history.

◎ Your innate tendencies.

Want to help your people better?
Help yourself.

Who Needs
You Now

You need more of The Right Clients – and you need them quickly. To land them, you need to focus your limited time and resources on nurturing those people who really need your help.

Below are three questions to ask your people to determine who has a need, who needs *you* and who needs you *now*.

1. Who has a need: 'What's the biggest problem you have with your [insert what you help with] right now?'

2. Who needs you: 'How hard has it been for you to find a meaningful answer to this problem?'

3. Who needs you now: 'How much of a difference would it make if this problem was solved for good?'

You can ask these questions in person, on a call, on email, or on a survey.

Here's how:

◎ Ask your people the three questions.

◎ Review their answers, particularly to question two.

For those who say it hasn't been particularly hard to find a meaningful answer, put them in the 'Do not contact' pile. They may have identified a need you can help with, but they are still in the explorer stage. The point of this exercise is to focus on those who need your help now and are the most likely to become clients now.

Review the answers to question two again. Look for those who gave you a longer answer, and particularly those infused with emotion. They are as ready as you're going to get.

Channel your resources to speak with these people first. They are in the decider stage – one stage away from purchaser.

Help them to see that you provide a meaningful answer for them, showing them the impact you've had on the lives of others and giving them the opportunity to ask you questions.

Now they are in purchaser stage. Make them an offer they can't refuse. They need you, now.

Stay On The Wagon

If you want to lead The Right Clients to work with you, you need to understand their journeys. Trying to build a business without this understanding is putting the cart before the horse. Here are three questions to get you on track with your business and keep the wheels turning in the right direction.

What's the wagon that your people find themselves repeatedly falling off?

It may not be that the wagon has stopped entirely. It could look like less focus, less fun, or less fulfilment.

That might be:

- ◎ The consistency wagon.

- ◎ The motivation wagon.

- ◎ The confidence wagon.

- ◎ The focus wagon.

Understand these roadblocks, and you will move toward figuring out the behavioural cycles of your people, which is the foundation for everything.

Why do your people keep falling off this wagon?
This is about understanding what happens that causes them to fall off the wagon. Think about:

- ◎ What happens in their mind?

- ◎ What happens in their life?

- ◎ What happens in their behaviours?

- ◎ What happens in their environment?

- ◎ What happens in their habits?

Understand why this is happening over and over and you'll be able to speak to their souls in your marketing.

What helps your people get back on the wagon?
Each time they fall off the wagon, they try a few things to get back on.

◎ What do they try?

◎ Why do they try it?

◎ What doesn't work?

◎ Why doesn't it work?

◎ What does work?

◎ Why does it work?

You'll find that it's the same thing that makes your people fall off the wagon each time, and the same thing that gets them back on it each time.

Understand what is happening, and you'll be able to give them what they need to stay on track and reach their goals.

Put all this together and you've got the fundamental understanding of your clients that will meaningfully drive both your business model and your marketing.

The Answers
Don't Change

Before you offer any new services to the world, ask yourself these questions:

◎ What do my T1s truly need?

◎ What do my T1s come to me for?

◎ What makes me the right fit for my T1s?

◎ How do I show my T1s that I understand them?

◎ How do I get my T1s to accept where they're at?

◎ How do I get my T1s to embrace the path?

◎ How do I empower my T1s to express themselves fully?

Because whatever the product or service, these answers don't change.

In order to create the right service for The Right Clients as well as for you and your business, be sure you get the answers to these questions right.

Help Everyone, Help No One

A business model that tries to help everyone is a business model that helps no one.

A business model that tries to help everyone leads to fatigue for you, because you're running around trying to keep everyone happy. You're constantly thinking of how to improve, but there's just too much to work on. You constantly feel like you need to add value, because you want to keep your clients happy.

A business model that tries to help everyone leads to frustration for the client, because it doesn't specifically serve their needs. This is the age of individualisation and personalisation. Generic solutions simply don't cut it anymore. People are used to getting what they want, how they want it, when they want it.

Your offerings aren't targeted enough to give them the deep value they crave.

So you always feel they are on the edge of leaving. Because they are.

This business model ultimately leads to failure, because it's impossible to focus your strategy, implementation or communication.

A business model that leads The Right Clients the right way is the intersection of:

◎ A business model that leads your people the right way.

◎ A business model that leads you the right way.

◎ A business model that takes your business the right way.

The solution is focus and personalisation. But it's a myth that personalisation comes from presenting loads of options. That leads right back to fatigue, frustration and failure.

Personalisation is best achieved through knowing who The Right Clients are.

And understanding them well enough to create a series of specific, sharp offerings that give them exactly what they need. A path that leads them from where they are, to exactly where they want to be.

Align Your Decisions

The more successful you and your business become:

◎ The more you'll be inundated with infinite ideas.

◎ The more you'll be plagued by permutations of possibilities.

◎ The more opportunities and options will open up to you.

This gives rise to a lot of decisions. Below are some questions to help you make these the right, aligned decisions for you and for your clients:

Have you locked in your values and vision?
Does your decision align with your values?
Does your decision align with your vision?

Have you determined your strategy and priorities for the weeks and months ahead?
Does your decision align with your strategy?
Does your decision align with your priorities?

Have you profiled your clients, their needs and your strengths?

Is your decision aligned with what you do best as a business?

Is your decision aligned with what your clients actually need?

Have you solidified and future-proofed your offering?

Is your decision aligned with what you currently offer?

Is your decision aligned with what you want to offer?

Have you planned the communications you want to create?

Does your decision align with the journey into your offering?

Does your decision align with the rest of your marketing?

Once you have your answers, you'll know what to do.

◎ Align your decisions and you'll align your business.

◎ Align your business and you'll align your people.

◎ Align your people and you'll align your life.

Create The Right Thing

When you create for The Right Clients,
you create the right thing.

When you create for the wrong clients,
you create the wrong thing.

Create for the
'Let's change things.'
Not for the
'Stop changing things.'

Create for the
'I want to hear what he thinks.'
Not for the
'I'm worried about hearing what he thinks.'

Create for the
'I've got your back.'
Not for the
'I won't come back.'

Create for the fist-pumpers.
Not for the fist-shakers.
Create for the T1s.
Not for the T3s.

Create the right thing for The Right Clients.
Not for the right thing for the wrong clients.

The **Starving Artist**

It's time to banish the myth of the starving artist. It's a myth that holds many of us back without us realising, and it goes a little something like this: if you do creative, meaningful, and fulfilling work, you'll never make any money.

This leads us to think:

◎ That making creative things and making money are mutually exclusive.

◎ That work that fills your soul can't possibly fill your wallet.

◎ That work that is emotionally rewarding can't be financially rewarding.

This holds us back from stepping into the Work Worth Doing, the work that we really want to do. Because we think we'll have to sacrifice financial reward for emotional reward.

If you merely pour your heart out onto a canvas or page, or you pour your resources into a business on a whim, you may well end up as the starving artist. Understand this fundamental truth: every successful creative endeavour begins with understanding and serving the deep needs of your people. The people who you can touch, help and serve the most. Personal fulfilment comes from serving the deep needs of other humans with our deep human strengths.

All successful artists make art that helps people explore the deepest problems of society and the human condition, through talent and work that compels people to explore those issues for themselves. When you realise that the process of successful and soulful creation isn't mere whimsical artistry, but careful crafting based on understanding the people you can help most, exploring their deepest issues and meeting their needs through the craft that you are best at...

... you'll be ready to step into Work Worth Doing, knowing that your work gives your clients deep value and aligns with your own values and value, and so takes you toward being emotionally *and* financially valued.

And that is a truly beautiful picture.

The Bad, The Good, The Great

'Sell them what they want.
Give them what they need.'

If you follow this advice, you are setting yourself up for disaster, through misaligned perceptions and mismatched expectations.

In place of that, consider this:

- A bad coach gives clients what they want.

- A good coach gives clients what they need.

- A great coach gets clients to want what they need.

Instead of selling them what they want, communicate in a way that gets The Right Clients to want what they need.

The Right Spot

Do you want your marketing to speak to The Right Clients? That starts with assessing where you're at with your marketing now.

Ask yourself the questions below about your marketing. Answer them instinctively and truthfully.

◎ Does it connect with The Right Clients and their deep needs?
Or does it miss the mark and feel disconnected?

◎ Does it feel like a true representation of you and the business?
Or does it feel like you are putting content out just because you should?

◎ Does it take people on a feel-good journey into your business?
Or does it simply provide information with an occasional 'sell'?

  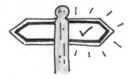

◎ Does it position your work as meaningful next steps?
Or does your offer feel like a push?

◎ Does it align with your offering?
Or is there a disconnect between marketing and offering?

◎ Does it have goals and milestones?
Or is it random and rambling?

◎ Is it enjoyable, even cathartic to create?
Or is it stressful and painful to create?

◎ Does it have space to be creative and connective?
Or is it standard and generic?

◎ Does it reflect your value and values?
Or does it fall short of your work and your worth?

◎ Does it bring in The Right Clients?
Or does it bring in a mix, many of whom end up being the wrong clients?

Marketing that delivers the right message, at the right time, in the right way, hits the right spot with The Right Clients.

Create The Clients

It's not about more clients.
It's about more of The Right Clients.

Rarely does The Right Client magically appear
as the result of one paid ad or promoted post.
You'll get leads, sure. But if a lead happens to be
The Right Client for your business, it's more by
chance than by skill.

Why would you leave that to chance?

If you haven't taken the time to build a relationship
through connective, consistent content that takes
people on a journey from never having heard of you,
to understanding the problem, to seeking a solution,
to finding the right help, to seeing that *you* are the
right help...

... then you are leaving it to chance.

If you want more of The Right Clients, you need to:

◎ Create meaningful content that compels
   the right people and repels the wrong ones.

◎ Start meaningful conversations that build
   rapport and dig into deep needs.

◎ Lead into meaningful consultations that result in a roadmap to solving those problems.

◎ Secure conversions that feel right and richly rewarding for all.

Do the above, and you'll get clients who love what you do, understand why you do it and stick around to enjoy it.

Meaningful Marketing

Meaningful marketing is about leading people, not telling people.

Meaningful marketing is about meeting people where they are at, not meeting people where you are at.

Once you understand:

- ◎ Who you are.

- ◎ Who your people are.

- ◎ What they truly need.

- ◎ How you deeply meet those needs.

It's then about:

- ◎ The right message.

- ◎ To the right people.

- ◎ In the right way.

- ◎ At the right time.

Here's a six-stage communications framework for you to filter all your marketing through.

Stage 1
You know that thing you've been told?
Here's the perspective shift.

Stage 2
You know that problem you're facing?
Here's the real issue at hand.

Stage 3
You know that outcome you want?
Here's the best way to get there.

Stage 4
You know what's available to you?
Here's a chance for you to try it out.

Stage 5
You know you need my help?
Here's a meaningful offer for you.

Stage 6
You know that you are valued?
Here's a unique opportunity for you.

Take your core messaging and filter it through these layers of communication. Repeat these stages in weekly, monthly and quarterly cycles. You'll find it leads people on a meaningful journey to a mutually fulfilling outcome. And for The Right Clients, that outcome is working with you.

Why Your People
Aren't Buying

Start by asking yourself:

◎ Is this the right person?

◎ Is this the right thing?

◎ Is this the right time?

These are big questions.
Take your time answering them.

If the answers are yes, yet your people aren't buying consider which of the following spectrums are at play.

The Value–Price Spectrum

People buy on value,
not price.

Know your people,
and know what they value.

◎ Was the value to them enough to justify
   the price?

◎ Was the value important enough to them
   to justify the price?

◎ Was the value communicated well enough
   to justify the price?

The Risk–Reward Spectrum

There are risks that come with choosing to
be supported.

The returns and rewards need to be greater than
the risks.

◎ Have you mitigated the risk safely enough?

◎ Have you positioned the return powerfully enough?

◎ Have you communicated the reward
   meaningfully enough?

The Challenge–Support Spectrum

Too much challenge with too little support, and people get scared.

Too little challenge with too much support, and people get bored.

- ◎ Was the challenge in the offer too great?
- ◎ Was the challenge in the offer too small?

- ◎ Was the support in the offer too much?
- ◎ Was the support in the offer too little?

Discounting Is
Dangerous

In difficult times, it can be tempting to discount.

To drop prices in order to 'win business'.

But let's draw an analogy here. You know that client who pops up once in a while, desperately wants to do everything all at once, then disappears, until the next time?

It's too little, and at the same time, too much. It lacks authenticity, sustainability and longevity.

Discounting is the marketing equivalent of that client. Often, businesses resort to discounting when there hasn't been enough of a meaningful marketing build up. These are the last businesses who should be discounting in an attempt to win business.

When there hasn't been a meaningful marketing build up before the discount, we attract the wrong people.

Meaningful marketing, when done well, compels The Right Clients and repels the wrong people. But when we don't have that, we are reinforcing the behaviours we don't want – seeking value through price.

And it gets worse from here.

Client retention is meant to be more effective, and more cost effective, than client acquisition. But when you start your relationship based on a discount, retention becomes expensive. You have to 'buy' your client again, either through continued or further discounts, or by giving them the world. Yet still they are not happy, because they want the world, but cheaper.

When you do meaningful marketing and build relationships over time, you get The Right Clients and everything feels easy. They understand you. They roll with the punches in the business. They are the first to get involved with new things. They spread the word to their friends.

When you give discounts, for instant sales and gratification, you get the wrong clients and everything feels difficult. You always feel that you're fighting an uphill battle. They don't like changes. They are the first to complain. They spread the word to their friends.

You choose.

Make A **Difference**

If you want to make a difference to your people,
be different.

Building a meaningful, impactful business is about
creating meaningful, unique solutions to solve unmet
client dilemmas. That means thinking differently
and finding ways to help your people that serve their
unmet needs in a way they haven't encountered yet.

This comes from two places:

First, you need to look at your people and their
dilemmas differently.

Be unwilling to accept that how most of your people
currently solve their dilemmas:
is the only way to solve their dilemmas,
is the best way to solve their dilemmas,
is even a good way to solve their dilemmas.

Why do you think most of your people keep looping
around the same dilemmas in health, business and
life, again and again?

Second, you need to look at yourself and your uniqueness differently.

Be unwilling to believe that how most of your competitors currently serve their clients:
is the only way to serve their clients,
is the best way to serve their clients,
is even a good way to serve their clients.

Why do you think most of your competitors keep looping around the same issues in their health, business and life, again and again?

If you want to make a difference to your people, be different.

That means getting outside your head.
That means thinking differently.

That means surrounding yourself with people:
who march to a different drum,
who dance to different tune,
who sing a different song.

You'll find yourself looking at life and business differently.

You'll find yourself looking at your clients differently.

You'll find yourself looking at your uniqueness differently.

You'll find yourself thinking differently.

You'll find yourself working differently.

You'll find perspectives you hadn't considered yet.

You'll find insights that change the game.

Put those pieces into action in your work and words and you'll find yourself in a different place when it comes to your life and your business.

If you want to make a difference to your people, be different.

You Get
What You Give

If you are not getting what you need from your people, give that to them.

If you need something more from your people, show them what that looks like.

If you need your people to interact with you differently, make that change with them.

If you want your people to be more open, be more open with them.

If you want your people to be more engaged, be more engaged with them.

If you want your people to be more respectful, be more respectful of them.

If you want better from your people, show them better from yourself.

FOUR

The Right
Support

The Right Thing

The thing we need most help with is the thing we help others with most.

Remember, your best clients are The Right Clients. And The Right Clients are previous versions of you.

The reason you are so incredible at helping your clients isn't because you have it all figured out.

The reason you are so incredible at helping your clients is because you haven't got it all figured out.

It's *because* you haven't got it all figured out, not *despite* that you haven't figured it all out, that you can powerfully help your clients.

You only need to be two levels ahead of your clients. You need to be only *two* levels ahead of your clients. And you need to *stay* two levels ahead of your clients.

This means seeking help with the thing you help others with most. Because this is the thing *you* need help with most.

There is no shame to be found in that. In fact, there is pride, joy and fulfilment to be found in that.

It's your responsibility to ensure you give the right support to the right people.

It's also your responsibility to ensure that you get the right support, to support your people.

Because you are the right people.

The Right Support

The thing that is stopping you from embracing
the support you need is the thing that you need
support with.

This is true for your people.
And this is true for you.

But what does it mean?

If confidence is stopping you from embracing
the support you need, confidence is the thing you
need support with.

Support to keep the imposter monster in his box,
to connect with your uniqueness and value and
show you that this comes from your unique values.

Support to start expressing yourself, authentically
and unapologetically.

To put yourself out there, powerfully.

If fear is stopping you from embracing the support you need, fear is the thing you need support with.

Support to show you it's possible, that it's possible for you and that it's your time.

Support to start making decisions from a place of possibility.

To find excitement in the possibilities.

If money is stopping you from embracing the support you need, money is the thing you need support with.

Support to understand your individual money story, to meet you where you are at, to both practically and mentally help you to rewrite your story.

Support to start making more money, meaningfully.

To become emotionally and financially valued.

If time is stopping you from embracing the support you need, time is the thing you need support with.

Support to see what is taking up your time but giving you little back, to help use your newfound time in a focused and fulfilling way and to build a business that supports that.

Support to be present for the important people.

To find time for those who matter – and that includes you.

The thing that is stopping you from embracing the support you need is the thing that you need support with.

What's stopping you from embracing the support you need?

The Right
Challenge

We're told to surround ourselves with people like us. People who are the same as us. People who share the same perspective.

But we're also told to surround ourselves with people unlike us. People who are different to us. People who can show us different perspectives.

Which is the right way? Who are the right people?

The right people are those who align with your values and boost your vision but challenge your views.

The right people are those who align with your worldview and boost your viewpoint but challenge your point of view.

The right people are those who challenge and support in equal measure.

Here's my advice for who to avoid and who to seek when it comes to finding the challenge and support that you need.

Avoid:

◎ Those who challenge you just to get you to work with them.

Seek:

◎ Those who support you in the moment. Challenge and support must exist in equal measure.

Avoid:

◎ Those who challenge you aggressively and ask for this to be received with action and immediacy.

Seek:

◎ Those who challenge you respectfully and ask for this to be received with reflection and honesty.

Avoid:

◎ Those who push you to make a decision in their favour, regardless of your circumstances.

Seek:

◎ Those who challenge and support you to make the right decision, for you, right now, whatever that may be.

Avoid:

◎ Those who are elusive, uncontactable and unapproachable.

Seek:

◎ Those who are engaged, connected and human.

Avoid:

◎ Those who are simply 'motivational'.

Seek:

◎ Those who are inspirational.

Avoid:

◎ Those who promise individualised support,
but produce standardised outcomes for
their people.

Seek:

◎ Those who have systemised support that creates
individualised outcomes for their people.

Find this challenge and support and you'll find
your way to a place of confidence, connection and
creativity – and beyond.

The Right
Resources

The right resources help the right people to do the right things, in the right way.

If you'd like to read more insights like those in this book, join the Facebook group at www.realign.global/group.

If you'd like additional resources to help you answer the questions in this book, access the supporting materials at www.realign.global/resources.

If you'd like to learn how well you know your market, complete the online diagnostic at www.realign.global/diagnostic.

And if you'd like to join a workshop to get clear on the next steps and ask questions, check out upcoming events at www.realign.global/events.

Acknowledgements

I am thankful to have the right people
right at the heart of my life.

Thankful for my wife, Jules.
Thankful for her unwavering support.
Thankful for her unconditional love.
Thankful for her undying belief.
Thankful for her.

Thankful for my dad, Nilesh, and my mum, Bindi.
Thankful for all the sacrifices they have made for me.
Thankful for always telling me that I could be anyone I
wanted to be.
Thankful for being there at every turn with me.
Thankful for them.

Thankful for my boys, Hilton and Laurence.
Thankful for the love we share.
Thankful for the family we are.
Thankful for the boys they are.
Thankful for the men they are becoming.

Thankful to my family and friends.
Thankful for family.
Thankful for friendship.
Thankful for where these converge.

Thankful for everyone who supported my first book, *Work Worth Doing*.

Thankful for your support for this book, too.

Thankful to everyone who contributed to this book.

Thankful for the observations, conversations and inspiration.

Thankful for my publishers, Rethink Press.

Thankful for Lucy, Joe and Eve.

Thankful for their endless wisdom and dedication.

Thankful for Roger, Anke and Jennifer.

Thankful for their review and organisation.

Thankful for my illustrator, Jon.

Thankful for his talent and creativity.

Thankful for his professionalism and responsibility.

Thankful for all my clients, mentors and partners.

Thankful that they give me permission to be honest with them at all times.

Thankful that they feel that they can be raw, open and honest with me.

Thankful that they allow me to challenge hard and support deeply, always with respect.

Thankful for the respect they give to me, to boundaries and to the process.

Thankful that they empower me with the responsibility to do more than my part in our work.

Thankful that they feel empowered to take responsibility for more than their part in our work.

Thankful to be able to navigate our work, and this world with them.

With the right people, everything works.

The Illustrator

Jon Jack's artistic journey began in Oxfordshire, where he grew up. His passion for illustration started at home, often drawing monsters and other content that was a little beyond his years!

Jon's playful yet striking illustrations mirror Chet's approach to writing. Their mutual connection and respect are evident throughout the book. The illustrations are a collaboration of two inventive minds working together to generate visual concepts that enhance connection with the words.

His supportive partner Susie and two young children, Joe and Arnie, provide Jon with inspiration for more of the illustrations than they could ever realise.

🌐 www.jonjacksillustration.com

The Author

 **Chet Morjaria** is a business and communications coach, and founder of Realign Global.

Realign Global coaches entrepreneurs who love what they do but struggle to create meaningful offerings and marketing that are a true reflection of their value and values. Chet has taught hundreds of coaches and business owners to do this over the last decade.

Chet works best at the intersection of meaningful work and powerful words. For over five years he ran a successful coaching business, teaching coaches how to communicate powerfully and meaningfully with clients. He has spoken on doing work with meaning and creating powerful communications at top industry summits.

His previous roles include Global Managing Editor for Breaking Muscle, a health and fitness website, where he managed six editors and two hundred writers to create daily content for eight million monthly visitors.

He currently lives in Berkshire, UK, with his wife, Jules, and their two boys, Hilton and Laurence.

What makes this Work Worth Doing to Chet is when his clients, The Right Clients, feel deeply aligned to their work, their words and their world.

🌐 www.chetmorjaria.com

f chetmorjaria
in chetmorjaria

🐦 chetmorjaria
📷 chetmorjaria

Lightning Source UK Ltd.
Milton Keynes UK
UKHW021956190122
397397UK00008B/249

9 781781 336526